"Facebook for Network Marketers:

Learn How to Increase Your Sales

Exponentially"

Harwood E. Jones

"Facebook for Network Marketers: Learn How to Increase Your Sales Exponentially" © 2016 Harwood E. Jones

All Rights Reserved.

Table of Contents

Introduction 4

Chapter 1 Facebook Basics 6

Chapter 2 Creating a Facebook Profile or Page 9

Chapter 3 What Type of Content to Post to Facebook 15

Chapter 4 The Benefits of Facebook Groups 23

Chapter 5 The Use of Facebook Ads 30

Chapter 6 How to Direct Facebook Traffic to a Website 42

Conclusion 44

Introduction

As a network marketer, when you wake up in the morning you may ask yourself how can you build better relationships with your clients or what you can do to build new relationships with potential clients. There are many ways to do this. Some are old school like being nice or speaking at events. These ways might still work, but the impact they have is reduced to a small number of listeners. Compared with the new methods the Internet era created, those ways are inefficient.

Online advertising, emails, websites and social media allow you to reach billions of people. You are no longer limited to people near you. When businesses are looking to have a global impact, they no longer waste money on old and inefficient ways.

One of the most effective social media for your business to have an impact among people is Facebook. It has the broadest range of options out there. Whether you are just starting out with network marketing or a giant MLM corporation, Facebook allows you to target a wide range of people. You can set up your Ads to target a small niche or the whole world population if needed. The opportunities are practically endless.

The social networking giant has more than 1.7 billion profiles. That means that your target audience probably has a Facebook profile.

In this book we will discuss the tools Facebook offers to engage your audience, how you can use Facebook strategically to target certain niches, what are Facebook Events and Groups and how to create them, how to direct Facebook traffic to your website, and ultimately make a sale. Although all of this might not look easy, after finishing this book you will have perfect knowledge and you will be able to reach millions of people that will be interested in your product.

<u>Why Facebook is so powerful?</u>

You may be use to sending direct emails to attract new customers. The problem with this is that you can't be absolutely sure that the person receiving the email will actually be interested in your business. Facebook lets marketers engage people in a new dimension.

With Facebook marketing, you can take advantage of your customers by them telling their friends through Facebook about your business. As you may know, word of mouth is really powerful in advertising. Also, Facebook is really powerful because it allows you to target people that are already talking about something related to your product or industry.

Facebook has billions of connected users, leveraging this connectivity lets you engage with people through creative content that will make your business stand out and lead to thousands of new clients for your product.

Chapter 1 Facebook Basics

Do you remember how your life was before Facebook existed? Maybe you used the Internet to send an email to a friend, or read about a certain topic. But, to keep up with your close social circle, you had to meet them for a talk or call them over the phone. With the creation of Facebook this changed forever. You are now able to keep up with a lot of people at the same time on one place. You now get updates of your friend being promoted or photos from your sister's baby all in your news feed. This is the power of Facebook. It helps keeping people connected.

What is Facebook?

Facebook is the most popular social network for connecting with people. Everything from status updates to personal photos is posted to Facebook and most of it is available for your friends to see (You can change your privacy settings to change this). You can send messages to any profile and chat. The site is available in more than 35 languages. It includes features such as:

1. Marketplace, which allows people to post, read and to answer classified Ads.
2. Groups, which allows people with common hobbies or interest to find each other and interact.
3. Events, which allow people to create an event, make it public and invite people.
4. Pages, which allows people to create a specific public page to promote a certain thing

Each personal profile contains a wall where friends can see your most recent posts, photos and videos. Also, they can post messages to your wall.

Facebook also has a News Feed which showcases real time interactions that occur between your friends, friends of friends and Pages. This can be used in favor of your business, because when someone comments something on your post, a real time update will be seen by everyone who has this "someone" as a friend. This makes networking much easier.

Facebook can be accessed through your phone and your pc.

Some Facebook Statistics

I will list some of Facebook's current statistics to help you visualize how big and helpful this social network is:

-1.79 billion users, increasing over 15 percent year after year (Source: Facebook)

-4.5 billion likes generated daily (Source: Facebook)

-Ages 25 to 34 dominates Facebook's demographics with 30 percent of the user base (Source: Emarketer 2012)

-Five new profiles are created every second (Source: ALLFacebook 2012)

-Highest traffic is from 1 to 3 PM (Source: Bit.ly blog)

-On Thursdays and Fridays traffic increases over 15 percent (Source: Bit.ly blog)

-300 million photos a day (Source: Gizmodo)

-4.75 billions of posts shared daily (Source: Facebook)

-Every 60 seconds on Facebook: 510 comments are posted, 293,000 statuses are updated, and 136,000 photos are uploaded. (Source: The Social Skinny)

-Over 40 percent of Marketers report that Facebook is critical for their business (Source State of inbound Marketing)

Do you see the impact you can achieve through using Facebook for marketing your product?

For example, let's say a popular local pastry shop doesn't use Facebook. They will be missing a lot. While many clients will talk about the local shop to a couple of people, many of its clients are taking pictures of the awesome looking pastries and posting them to Facebook. Most of the shop's customers and potential customers are using Facebook. So, it is therefore a must that the coffee shop creates its own Page where they can engage customers directly, comment on their photos, making offers to them and ultimately increasing the amount of people they impact. All of the new clients that the shop would lose if it hasn't created Facebook are too big. Then, the pastry shop can post updates saying things like: "Post photos of your pastries to Facebook this week for a chance of earning a dozen of pastries FREE". This is one of the ways Facebook can be used.

An example more related to network marketing is someone who sells let's say Avon products in a certain state. Using Facebook, he/she will be able to set up Ads for people who are interested in this industry, as well as setting up a radius of 20 miles for the Ad to show up. The Ad will only appear to people that are really potential customers. By doing this he /she now has thousands of soon-to-be clients that might contact him and buy his/her product. We will expand more on this in Chapter 4.

According to Zephoria.com, Facebook user base is growing by approximately 15 percent every year. Emarketer also affirmed that over 15 percent of adults search Facebook before purchasing something. This means that having a good Facebook Page might potentially make or break a sale decision. Developing a business Page is certainly essential for network marketing and really **any** business.

Chapter 1 Key Points:

- Facebook connects more than 1.5 billion people. Your target market is absolutely using Facebook daily.
- By not using Facebook to promote your business, you are losing a lot of potential customers.
- Network marketers can really benefit a lot from Facebook. You can really expect to increase your sales by a huge number. Your number of connections will increase exponentially.

Chapter 2 Creating a Facebook Profile or Page

Should I Create a Profile or a Page?

If you are a network marketer and just starting out with social media marketing, you might have asked yourself this very question. In the following paragraphs, I will try to explain the differences in the best possible way.

The main difference between a profile and a page in Facebook is that profiles are for personal, non-commercial use and represent a single person. When you use a profile and want people to be able to see your posts, you need them to add you as a friend. The main problem with this is that there is a limit to the amount of friends a profile may have (5000 friends). Once you reach this limit, people are able to follow your profile and be able to see your public updates. Some people may hesitate following a personal profile because it doesn't show the same level of professionalism a page offers.

Also, if you are going to represent a business, Pages are a must. You cannot use a personal profile to represent something that is not a person because it is against Facebook terms. Doing so may cause potential access loss to your account.

Pages are not that different to a profile in the way you post your public updates. Pages are handled by people with personal profiles. The good thing is that people can follow you in a much simpler way and there is no limit to the amount of people that can follow your updates. Following a page in Facebook is given the famous name of "Liking". When you like a page, you are basically following it. People that like a page will become your Page's fan. Fans will receive all the updates the Page posts in their news feed. Pages are specifically made for businesses, organizations and brands. They contain exclusive tools made to simplify all of the actions one would carry out when promoting his brand.

One of the features that allow you to have more control over your updates is called Page insights, where you are able to see stats like which posts are your fan's favorites and visitor demographics like location and age.

By using a Page, you can assign specific people to access and manage your Page by using Page roles. This person can edit your page the same way as you do.

And most importantly, by using a Page you can create Ads and boost posts. This will increase the amount of people that see the Page. These Ads will appear to people when they are reading their news feed in the sides of the website/App. We will expand more on the usage of Ads to expand your business in Chapter 4.

Before you create your page, here are some guidelines that will help you plan your way into a successful Page:

- Know your objective, how will you position yourself, and what Tone will you use in your posts.
- Fill out all the Page sections. Be sure to get images in the highest quality possible to set up as profile picture and cover photo. Include your website link so that people can get to your site.
- Be engaging with your audience. Your posts should be appealing and fun for your target audience. Your fans want to have a good time when reading their news feed. Try to encourage them to comment on your posts. And reply to all customers!
- Plan when you are going to share and what. There might be certain hours your target audience is more active. For example, if your target audience is kids you might want to schedule your posts for the most common lunch hours.

So to let this issue perfectly clear, I will give you some examples of Facebook Pages: Coca-Cola, Apple, Mashable, Nike,

Oprah, Taylor Swift, New York Mets, Massachusetts Institute of Technology.

Setting up Your Page

Creating a page is really simple, you just have to go to www.facebook.com/pages/create and select the appropriate category for your page. The categories include: Local business or place; Company, Organization or Institution; Brand or Product; Artist, Band or Public Figure; Entertainment; And Cause or Community. If you are network marketing a certain product, you will need to choose either Local business; or Brand or Product.

If for some reason you have already created a personal profile to represent your business, Facebook allows you to convert your profile into a Page. This creates a new Facebook Page that's based on your personal account. This can be done only once. So pay attention in the future if you want to represent your business.

What will happen after you convert your Facebook profile into a Page?

- You will have a personal account and a Page
- Facebook will transfer your cover photo and profile picture to the Page
- The name of the profile will be shared
- You can access this new Page from within your personal account.

We have already seen why having a Facebook page is a must. But, if the Page is not set up correctly, it will be useless.

Designing a Facebook Page is really easy. Anyone can create his Page in some minutes, but it takes some planning and tinkering to make your Page right for business and to encourage its visitors to carry out a specific action. You, as network marketer might want to sell your product in a certain area or recruit more people to sell your product. By setting it up correctly, visitors will be much more receptive to your goals.

You will need to fill the most information you can. What should you be filling?

- Description: This will enable visitors to understand better the product you are selling. This is very similar to the "about" page you set up on your website. Having a good description can make or break someone liking your page and be interested in your product.
- Include your website if you have one, this might be useful for customers that want to become more informed on your product or if you are selling the product online.
- Profile picture: Here you have to add a good looking, attractive photo. It can be either a LOGO or a photo of your product. When you start using Ads people will see your profile picture in the Ad.
- Cover photo: Also really important. This photo is bigger and clients will see it on top of your Page. You will want a picture that really represents your business. Like, for example, a picture of your best sold product. Also, you can add text to your cover photo. You can include a call to action: "contact me today for 10% off in X product".

As we mentioned some couple of pages before, you can name different people to help you manage your page. This people can hold different levels of responsibility. I will show you the different positions and their responsibilities in the following chart:

	Manager	Content Creator	Moderator	Advertiser	Insight Analyst
Manage admin Roles	Yes	No	No	No	No
Edit the Page and add Apps	Yes	Yes	No	No	No
Create posts as the Page	Yes	Yes	No	No	No
Respond and delete comments	Yes	Yes	Yes	No	No
Send messages as the page	Yes	Yes	Yes	No	No
Create ads	Yes	Yes	Yes	Yes	No
View Insights	Yes	Yes	Yes	Yes	Yes

Chapter 2 Key Points

- Personal profiles are for personal, non-commercial use
- Pages are specifically made for businesses. They contain many tools that will help you engage your audience
- Pages are a must for anyone that wants to expand their business network

- Designing a page is easy. You just need some creativity

Chapter 3 What Type of Content to Post to Facebook

Now that your Facebook page is finally set up, you might ask yourself what is the main reason to post content to your Facebook Page. You are not sharing just to make your fans laugh. You should be posting to engage and ultimately grow a bigger audience. And at some point this audience will become your best clients.

When someone engages with your posts, be a like, a comment, or a share. You are growing your audience. Firstly, it means that your audience is enjoying the content you are posting and are probably recommending their friends to like your Page. Secondly, when a person likes or comments on your video, these actions appear on their friends' news feed: "[X person] has liked [or commented] on [Y Page post]". Both of these really increase your impact on people. Your page will become much better known.

Why do people use Facebook? They need to belong and they have a need for self-presentation. Most people log into Facebook to: Like content, message their friends, consume good content, comment status updates, and see what their friends are up to (Research by the Boston University).

Like vs. Share

When someone likes your post it means that they support the content you published. The content people share often means something to them, forging a bond with what they shared. When someone shares something, they are sharing it with probably their whole family, friends, colleagues and bosses. So when they share something it is because they agree strongly. Shares are much more valuable to your Page, because they increase your reach by a lot for free.

Different Types of Content

You might be wondering what content engages your audience the most. On the next pages, we will try to be clear on what the best content is and how to manage it.

There are different types of content you can post to your Facebook page. There are three main content categories you can post:

1. Images
2. Videos
3. Text

Images

Single Images Posts that include only one Image engage your audience 120 percent more than the average post. Photos engage your audience and are really easy to see and understand in a couple of seconds. They are the best content to post for marketing purposes. Images take up a large portion of your audience news feed; they draw much more attention than a simple text post.

Take a look on your Facebook news feed and see how much better a photo draws your attention than a text post, or thumbnail from a shared URL when you share a website's URL, Facebook displays a small thumbnail of it. If you want to share an URL you can just include it in your image posts. Use photos that are focused on what you want your audience to see. Images with a lot of contrast look great against Facebook's white news feed. For even better engaging include a short text that tells a story that your users can relate. Also, including text over your Image is great. You can include a call to action. For example: "Like this post," for one option, and, "Share it," for the other.

Good single images that are proven to engage your audience:

- Quotes: People love reading quotes from important people.
- Fun facts
- Comics/cartoons: Apart from making your audience laugh, some cartoons will inspire them to voice their opinion (AKA comment).

Photo Albums posts that include a photo album engage your audience 180 percent more than the average post. They are great to promote a new line of products, sponsor an event, and photo galleries of similar content. They allow posting multiple images of similar things without annoying your fans.

Goal: The main goal is to engage your audience in either them liking, commenting or sharing your Image.

Videos

Posts that include a video have twice as many engagements than the average post. When posting a video keep it simple and no longer than 2-3 minutes. They are great to show how to do something or events.

Goal: Same as the Image posts, video posts should engage your audience.

Text

Texts are best if they are short. They work best when they are approximately 250 characters (or 3 lines). They generate 60% more likes, shares and comments than texts longer than 250 characters. The best text posts are the ones that are interactive with your audience. Good examples include polls or questions. These types of posts generate more than 90 percent more engagement than the average text posts. Text key points:

1. No more than 250 characters
2. Call to action before the 100 character mark
3. Use a good Image to draw attention

Goal: With text only posts your aim should be to get people to comment and express their thoughts.

Links

Link posts happen when you paste a URL as a text post. Facebook generates a small thumbnail and description of the website for you. As I mentioned before, the thumbnail looks pretty small. It is better to post a photo because it looks much better. But if you need to include your website in a place other than the description of your Page or as a text in an Image content post, then this is the only option.

Goal: To increase traffic to your site. Your primary goal should be to get your audience to click and visit your website. The text should be short (no more than 150 characters) and include a call to action. For example: "Check out this website! Number 2 is my favorite. What is yours?" But be careful in including too much information because your reader won't need to check out the link because you gave them all the info.

What other Type of Content Works for Business Pages?

Other good content that really draws attention are promotions and discounts. For example: "Like, comment and share X post for a chance of winning Y product". To engage your audience even more you should set a specific deadline for them to check your promotion or discount. This creates a sense of urgency which will make them act even faster.

Reward your Facebook audience by including exclusive deals that only people who follow you on Facebook get. Your fans will feel special and they will probably recommend their friends to follow your Page so they can get the benefits.

You should relate your products to events that are happening in the world. For example: Christmas, Halloween, Thanksgiving, big financial events, etc. Your content can be tailored to the specific event. When close to Christmas, or Thanksgiving, if you post an image related to it or offer a special discount for the season, your audience will be much more engaged.

A good way to keep a constant flow of posts is to have a calendar with ideas for the content you will share with your audience. This content calendar will not only help you to publish regularly, but also it will guarantee that your content strategy is well thought out. Be interesting and keep up with events happening in the world. Look for a frequency that works for you and works for your fans.

Once you have the content calendar, Facebook Pages allows you to administer time better by setting up scheduled publications. To schedule publications, you just have to click the clock on the lower left corner of your Page. Schedule your content for when most of your fans are connected. You can find out about this see the Statistics of your Page.

Now that you know the content that most engages your audience, what should you do? You may choose to produce this kind of content by yourself and share it Facebook. That would be fine. But what would be even better is that before you share anything; learn what your audience wants. You might feel your audience wants certain kind of posts, but if these posts are not generating the right amount of engagement, then you might need to re-think your strategy. The best method to re-think your strategy is to make sure you know your audience, analyze your statistics and test different types of content.

Giveaways

Giveaways are really good to grow your audience. You post a good image of your product for example, and make people tag a friend and share the image. This is good at all growth stages, but works better when your Page is not too well known. It will attract a lot of people. Everyone will start tagging their friends. The growth is exponential. These giveaways, apart from growing your audience, will increase brand loyalty.

When someone gifts you something you are compelled to return the gift in the future. When a business gifts you something, the customer will want to reciprocate. He/she will want to buy the product in return. Think. What valuable can you give away that will trigger a "WOW that was really thoughtful"? This will trigger the effect of them being more loyal with your brand as well as probably buying you something in return.

Analyzing Your Facebook's Page Statistics

As we mentioned before, if you are looking for the best time to publish your content, the best place to find out is through

Facebook Insight. A tool specifically designed for looking at your Page stats. In the next few paragraphs, we will discuss which insights you should consider the most.

When accessing the Insight tool you will see many different tabs. The tabs divide the stats in different categories. They include: posts, videos, people and actions on Page.

The posts tab: You will discover two graphs that illustrate the average number of people who saw *any* content on Facebook by hour and day of the week. Pay attention to the "any" in the last sentence, as these stats don't show how many people actually saw your posts, but instead how many people are navigating Facebook at a given time. This tab will help you determine when the best time to publish your content is.

Also, there is another section in the posts tab that is very useful. It is called "All posts published" analytics. This section lets you check your posts in reverse chronological order and analyze each post engagement. Inside it there is tool called "Engagement rate" that helps you understand your post success by calculating the percentage of people who viewed and reacted to your post (liked, commented or shared). If your content is viewed by a large amount of people but it has a low Engagement rate, the post is marked as "Low quality". Having too many low quality posts hurts your Page because the algorithm that chooses which posts appear on your fans news feed is highly affected displaying less your posts.

Facebook has recently introduced a new way to react to content called "Reactions" which lets you know how people feel about your post. These reactions include being: wow, sad, angry, in love and ha-ha. Tracking reactions lets you know what your fans feel about your content.

Next, there is another section in the posts tabs called "Post Types". It shows which of your posts produced the highest engagement for your Page.

The videos tab displays the number of views your videos had, amount of people who watched your video more than 10 seconds and a list of your best videos.

The video stats can be filtered by:

- The ones that have been seen by people organically and the ones that have been seen by people because you paid to advertise it.
- The ones that were auto played vs. the ones that people click to see it.
- The ones that were played only once vs. the ones repeated.

The people tab you can go to "people engaged" to view the demographics of your audience categorized by the ones that liked your Page, the ones you have reached with Ads, and the ones engaged.

These analytics let you view your audience you engage sorted by location, age, gender, and language. Knowing who your main audience is really helps you to plan the type of content you will publish

The actions on Page tab: Recently Facebook added the possibility to add a call to action button. It has up to eleven different actions, like call the business or booking an appointment. This tab allows you find out the amount of people that clicked this button, the demographics and if they clicked it from their pc or from their Smartphone.

In conclusion, use Facebook Insights to your advantage in planning strategically the content you will publish.

Chapter 3 Key Points:

- When someone engages with your post, you are increasing your audience.
- People share content they deeply relate with.

- Keep your text post short and interactive.
- Images are the best type of content.
- Use Facebook Insights to plan strategically the content you will publish.

Chapter 4 The Benefits of Facebook Groups

You might be thinking whether if it's better to create a Page or Group. But in reality, you should be using both. Facebook Groups and Pages can be best friends if used correctly. Through both of them you can stay ten times more connected with your audience. A Facebook Group allows you to have next level communication with fans.

To understand how these two are tied, let's first explain the differences between them.

Differences between Facebook Groups and Pages

We have already explained thoroughly what Facebook Pages are. If you want information on what a Facebook Page is refer to Chapter 2. So let's continue with what Facebook Groups are.

Pages were designed to be profiles for businesses, celebrities, etc. They are formed by a huge number of people. As they are so big, one to one communication with the business is very hard. On the other hand, a Group is a place for small group communication where people who share a common interest express their opinions on a certain subject. People join a group because they share a common cause. These may be having an issue or activity to organize, discuss certain subjects or share related content.

Being a network marketer, you can create a Facebook Group around certain people who are near you and would like to sell your product for you. In it you discuss more private information and give knowledge to others. Then, you would have a Page of your product. In the group you discuss matters with the people who work for you and in the Page you advertise in order to make your product better known.

Setting up Your Group's Privacy Settings

When you create a Facebook Group you are given the option to choose between it being Public, Private or Secret. In the following chart you will understand what each of these categories entitles.

Who can…?	Public	Private	Secret
Join	Anyone can join or be added by a current member	Anyone can ask to join or be added by an admin	Anyone, but they have to be added either by a current member or an admin
See the group's name	Anyone	Anyone	Members and former members
See who the group members are	Anyone	Anyone	Members only
Stories about the group on Facebook's news feed	Anyone	Members only	Members only
See the group's description	Anyone	Anyone	Members and former members
See the group's tags	Anyone	Anyone	Members and former members
See what members post in the group	Anyone	Members only	Members only
Find the group in search	Anyone	Anyone	Members and former members

Facebook Groups in Business

As we said, using Facebook Groups alongside your Page is highly beneficial to achieve much better communication with your audience. In business, this is essential to achieve the ultimate goal of increasing and building relationships with people.

Groups let you set up a cover photo which will reflect your business brand. Admins can change this with letting Facebook set it up for you with an image of all the profile photos of your group's members.

Unlike Pages, Groups have a feature that lets you and your members search for previous post. So if someone is asking a commonly asked question, you can tell them to search for previous posts discussing the same issue. The results that the search shows are posts that contain the given words in any part of it. The given words will be highlighted so they are easily found.

Some of the tools that Groups contain are:

- Events
- Files (you can upload or create any type of file)
- Notifications

The tools may come handy, but they are not the main reason you are using Groups for Business.

<u>Reasons to use Groups in Business</u>

1. Gather people who have similar interests

All of us really like to be with people who share common interests, right?

If your business offers a certain product or service, these products or services might have lots of people who want to discuss between themselves about them. For example, in the case of Network Marketing, there might be a "Herbalife" group where people might have doubts about the different protein tastes or why are they healthy products. All of these questions might arise and encourage conversation between people. A group is the best place to hold these types of conversations. You can answer their questions and let other people contribute too.

<u>Why is it beneficial for business?</u> As conversations become more interesting, members might want to invite their friends to the

Group. This translates into new possible clients or brand ambassadors to do the talking for you.

2. Become "friends" with brand ambassadors

Every business has loyal clients who love telling their friends about how great your product or service is. This people are called brand ambassadors. Giving them power to do the talking is really smart. You now have free advertisement, as well as testimonials for your product or service.

Dialogue within a Group will help you strengthen this connection between these loyal clients and you.

Also, for network marketing, groups are really great to communicate with people who want to sell your product. You can help your salespeople or discuss new ideas.

<u>Why is it beneficial for business?</u> Your brand ambassadors will now have a tool that reaches large amounts of people to tell your story.

3. Discuss new ideas with salespeople

You can discuss new ideas, help, and ask for your salespeople input through Groups. A good leader can create a Facebook group to promote new ideas and gain support.

<u>Why is it beneficial for business?</u> You can forge better relationships with your committee.

4. Easier to be seen in the news feed

When people join a group, they know that what is being discussed is relevant to them. It is easy to know as they joined because they wanted and can leave when they want to. Your audience wants to be personally connected to what is being discussed in Groups. Also, group members are more likely to see the posts because they receive a notification each time a new post is published; and if they have commented on a post each time someone comments, they will receive a new notification.

<u>Why is it beneficial for your business?</u> Better communication with your audience and salespeople.

5. Members are more willing to give their personal contact info

One of the main goals of using Facebook for marketing is to enhance your relationships with old and new clients. Are you trying to build your first email list? Using a Facebook Group is a good way to achieve this naturally.

One of the ways is to propose events or activities that require their email to sign up. Or you might ask for someone's email to discuss a more private matter. All of these are ways to get people onto your mail list.

People are much more predisposed to share their email, phone number or any other private information as they feel that in a group everyone knows each other and it's a safe place to do so.

<u>Why is it beneficial for your business?</u> Having more personal relationships with your customers enables you to:

- Receive better feedback from your clients.
- Add them to your email list, being able to send them relevant news on your products or services.
- Create even more brand ambassadors.

6. You can sell products through Facebook groups

In addition from being a great communication tool, Facebook Groups allow you to use them as a marketplace. You can post products for sale in it like in any other online marketplace. You can set its price, location, description and add photos.

<u>Why is it beneficial for your business?</u> You now have an additional place to sell your product/service. If the Group turns out to have a lot of members, you can sell a lot through it.

7. If you are a network marketer, you can add video training courses.

You might want your salespeople to watch certain educational videos that will help them and you make more sales. This can easily be shared within the Group's file system. They will be stored forever and can be easily referenced whenever you want to. With the option of keeping your Group secret, you can be sure this content is watched only by the people you want.

<u>Why is it beneficial for your business?</u> Your salespeople will have an easy way to instruct themselves and will result in more sales.

8. Establish expertise

By answering all of the questions people might have, you declare yourself someone who really knows what you are doing. When you help other you always receive back. Try to give the most amount of value you can.

<u>Why is it beneficial for your business?</u> You will be sure that people know you are knowledgeable in your product/service and its benefits. You can destroy your competition by doing this as you will be known as the best of certain field.

9. You now have a core following of people who trust you.

Let's say you have a thousand members in your Group, you now have a following! This is great for any business. You now have good feedback always. You had a new idea? You can see how a sample of people reacts. Do you want to launch a new product or service? These people trust you and will probably buy from you as soon as the product/service launches.

<u>Why is it beneficial for your business?</u> It is pretty clear why having a following is great for business, right? You now have a network of people!

Now that you know how helpful having a Business Group is, the only thing you need to do is being consistent in engaging with your members. This alone will set things in motion to achieve whatever your goal is. Try to encourage good discussions that you can contribute a lot. To not only provide value, but to show your expertise.

<u>Chapter 4 Key Points</u>

- You should have a Facebook Page AND a Facebook Group
- Facebook Groups allow you to communicate better with your audience
- Groups will help you and consolidate your business among your competition
- Groups will build you a following

Chapter 5 The Use of Facebook Ads

There are more than 1.5 billion people using Facebook. It has people from everywhere in the world, people who will be interested in your product or service and are actively looking for it. Sometimes these people who are actively searching for your products will need some extra help in finding your product or service. Others might still not know they are searching for something like your product or service. With the help of Facebook Ads, you can target these specific people. These, and only these, will see your Ads. Only the people who you know that can be interested. That is why Facebook Ads are one of the best out there: because they can be targeted to certain demographics!

Some of you may have a friend who keeps insisting that Facebook Ads do not work. They are probably saying this because they have read an article of someone who used Facebook Ads to promote his business and failed miserably. But, he probably was doing it wrong. Why were there over one million advertisers who spend more than eight billion dollars on Facebook Ads then? Since 2010, Facebook advertising has grown over 650 percent! There is a reason for these. In this Chapter you will learn how to properly use Facebook Ads.

Difference between Facebook Ads and Google Adwords

The main difference between the two is that using Google Adwords limits your product or service to people who are actively searching for it. They search for a keyword using Google search and your advertised page appears on highlighted on the top.

Firstly, there are a limited numbers of keywords you may enter in Google Adwords. What are keywords? Keywords are words people might search for. For example, let's say you search for "Hotels in Barcelona", Google will give you lists of pages who will help you book a Hotel in Barcelona. But, you want your Website to stand out. So, you pay Google to position your Website on the top.

Secondly, as I said, they are not targeted. People who have an interest won't just stumble upon your website. They need to search for it. And if you are lucky to have a product that a lot of people are searching for, then it might be worth it. But, if your product is something new, and innovating that people still don't have a clue about, Facebook Ads are much better: They are targeted for people who already might have an interest in you.

Facebook Ads are also getting better every year. Just a couple of months ago they introduced new features for targeting your audience even better.

Facebook recently acquired Instagram, so now Ads are stronger than ever. Your Facebook Ads will also show on people Instagram's feed. Your audience is now bigger!

So, are you convinced to use Facebook Ads for your business yet?

Some Definitions

Ad campaign: A Campaign consists of one or more Ad sets or Ads. You can choose the main objective for your campaign. You should create a campaign for each different objective.

Ad sets: Ad sets consist of one or more Ads. You can define your target audience, budget, schedule and placement. You should organize each of your Ad sets to target your audience.

Ads: The actual Advertisement for your product or service.

Setting up Your Facebook Ads Account

Now, you will learn how to setup your Facebook advertising account. You will also learn how to handle permissions, changing and knowing your spending limit and other useful information that will help you plan your Ads strategically.

The first thing you need to set up is your payment method. Facebook allows most credit cards, PayPal. Fill in all the information asked when setting up the Ad account settings. If you are from Europe, Facebook will ask you to fill in your vat information. You can also set up the currency you want to be billed in and your time zone. Be extra careful when filling this page as this information can't be changed in the future.

I suggest you to add a second payment method as well, because if for some reason your primary payment method fails, for example if your credit card reaches the monthly limit, your Ads will be paused until you can pay for them. Restarting them can be a boring process.

In the past, Facebook charged your payment method each time someone clicked your Ad. Now, Facebook introduced changes that you reach certain thresholds and you are charged each time you reach that amount. The amount your threshold can be varies depending for how long you have been using Facebook Ads. You will first start with a $25 threshold; you will be billed $25 each time you spend $25 on your Ads. As your payments are processed correctly, this threshold will increase in intervals to $50, $250, $500 up to $750.

Having a higher threshold doesn't affect your Ads. It just changes the amount of times you will be billed for the Ads so that your payment method invoice is shorter.

Facebook Ads have limits. Regularly this won't be an issue, but it is better to have the knowledge and possibly expect it and, ultimately, know how to solve it. The limits are:

1. 5000 Ads per account.
2. 1000 campaigns per account
3. 25 advertisement account per user.

If for some reason you reach any of these limits, all you have to do is delete your old Ads and campaigns.

Also, there existed a limit that set the maximum amount of money you could spend on your Ads daily. But with the introduction of thresholds, this limit has been removed.

There exists another limit that YOU can set. It is a limit that that totals the amount of money you want to spend in Facebook Ads for your account. By default, it is set to be unlimited. But, if for some reason you wish to limit it you can manage it from the "billing" page.

Another important thing to set up is the notifications you receive. You should always be checking how your Ad campaigns are performing. Receiving notifications is a great way to stay informed. But if they are set incorrectly they can flood your inbox! Changing notification settings is a must. In your account information you will find two sets of notifications triggers: One for your email and the other one for your In-Facebook notifications. Simply check or uncheck the boxes. You should disable the "Ad approved" notification as those can really flood your inbox; you should only receive the ones that notify you when your Ads are rejected. Set your notifications to receive the most important ones to your email and the least important ones to your In-Facebook notifications.

Ad Types for Each Objective

There are many different types of Ads you can create in Facebook. Before creating your first campaign, I will explain to you the different Ads available. Throughout all these years, Facebook has really adjusted its advertisement; no matter what you want to advertise, you will find the correct type of Ad for it!

Increasing Your Website's Traffic Ads

One of the purposes of creating a Facebook Ad is to deliver traffic to your website. This has the goal to get people to visit a certain landing page where they can buy your products, subscribe to your email list, etc; or just increase your site's audience.

These are the Ads you will want to use for getting people to visit your website:

Domain Ad these Ads are placed on the Facebook's right column, so it is not available for mobile users. This is one of the simplest Ads you can create. In this Ad you can set up a title, a short description and the link to be displayed. Statistically, it underperforms in terms of its click-through rate (CTR), but if you are short on budget it's a good Ad to have as they are the cheapest.

Page Post Link these Ads are placed on Facebook's right column or on your audience news feed. Also, they are supported in mobile devices and desktop. It's the most commonly used Ad type.

It's the best Ad type for promoting your website. These Ads consist of a big image that catches your audience attention (pick a good, high-contrast image) and a small description where you can explain what your product or service is all about. Statistically, these Ads perform really well. They also have the nifty side benefit of generating likes for your Facebook Page. A good way to increase the Ad's impact is to reply to the comments your audience leaves.

Increasing Sales and Leads for your Business Ads

If you want to advertise an e-commerce stores or a brand, Facebook allows you to show multiple products or services in the same single Ad.

Facebook has also an Ad where people can leave their email addresses without leaving Facebook itself. This is just plain awesome. People are much more convinced on leaving their email through Facebook than if they have to visit an "outside" website. The credibility is much higher also.

Multi-Product (Carousel): These ads appear on your audience's news feed. They are supported for people using their mobile devices or desktop. It was released on mid 2014. They are very useful for marketers looking to advertise multiple products or services at the same time. You can include up to five images each of them with a different title and one short description. For example, if you own a MLM where you sell multiple tableware objects, using this type of Ad is beneficial because you are able to showcase five of your objects at the same time on the same Ad.

Dynamic Product Ads (DPA): These Ads appear on Facebook's right column or on your audience news feed. They show on desktop and on mobile. They also consist of a big image and a title. But, these Ads are one of the best because they automatically target the people that might be interested in your product or service. They check on people past actions (cookies) and if they have searched for something related to your business, these Ads will show up automatically in their Facebook.

Lead Ads: These Ads are available both for desktop and mobile. They were introduced in 2015. These Ads are really awesome for getting people emails right inside Facebook. They also consist on an image, a title and a short description. When your audience clicks on the Ad a form pops up right there. People do not need to leave Facebook and visit an external website to sign up to your newsletter, for example. As you might have guessed, these Ads are great for lead generation.

Canvas: These ads are mobile only. Basically, they are *interactive* Ads. That is why they are only available in mobile devices. They look like a regular Ad with an image, title and short description. But, when someone clicks them they open a Canvas where can swipe, tilt, zoom in and out images. They are completely different in this sense than other Ads.

Engagement for your Page Ads

Whether your goal is promoting your business Page or promoting your existing Page posts to reach more people, Facebook Ads are a great way to do so. There are Ads specifically designed to issue the latter goals. Anyways, in all cases it is important to target the right audience.

Page Like These Ads are the best for solely increasing your Page likes. They appear on the right column or on the news feed and are available in both Desktop and Mobile. It features a big image with a short description. But, most importantly it features a highly visible call-to-action for user to like your Page by clicking the Ad. As always, it is very important to pick an image that will catch your target audience eye.

Page Post Photo These Ads are also featured on the right column or on your audience news feed. These Ads appear only to people who have liked your Page, so keep that in mind. They are available in both Desktop and Mobile. This Ad features the biggest space of them all. It has a huge space for a nice image as well as short description. If you pick the right image people will be engaging like crazy.

Page Post Video These Ads are similar to Page Post Photo Ads. The difference is that the promoted content is a video. Statistically, videos are the most engaging content of all. So if you can produce a great video that connects with your business principles, plus connecting with your audiences' you will get exceptional engagement rates.

Page Post Text I am just going to mention these types of Ads. In my opinion there is no reason to promote a text post as promoting a Page Post Photo drives much more engagement and is ultimately much more worth your money.

Installs for Mobile Apps Ads

These Ads are beneficial if you are using some kind of app to promote your MLM. If you are not using an app, skip this part because the goal of these Ads is to get installs for it.

Mobile App these Ads are really similar to the Page Like Ads in terms of how they look, but instead of having a CTA to like your page, they have a CTA button to install an app. They are only available for Mobile users. When using these Ads, you will be able to choose if you want them to appear on devices with iOS, Android or both; if you want to target people using tablets; and if you want to target people that are using WIFI.

Visitors for Your Event or Store Ads

The goal of these Ads is to lead people to your physical store or event. The results are hard to measure because they are offline. If used correctly, they can be successful.

Offer: These Ads appear on the right column or on the news feed, are available for both Desktop and Mobile. These are perfect for people who want to attract other people to their stores. It features a picture and short description. Plus, a call to action button that lets your audience get an offer to redeem personally on your store. If you can tailor your target audience to people near you that are interested in your business, you will get great results!

Event: These Ads appear on the right column or on the news feed, they are available for both Desktop and Mobile. Facebook events are awesome for organizers who want to attract visitors. If you want to increase the reach of your event these Ads are absolutely helpful. Remember to limit the geographical reach of the Ad to people near you.

As we are learning, Facebook has a different type of Ad for each goal you or your business might have. Pick strategically and don't be afraid to experiment and, using Ads statistics, determine which type of Ad is best.

Setting up Your First Ad

Now you are fully knowledgeable in setting up your first Ad account and the different Ad types that Facebook offers. What to do next? It is time to create your first Facebook Ad. Before even paying a dollar, you should have a clear purpose or goal to achieve with this Ad campaign. Think about this and once you have decided the purpose head to Facebook Ads Manager and click "create an Ad" button.

The first thing that Facebook asks you is what goal you want to achieve with your Ad. Here you will have a list which will include every different Ad type we have seen in the last paragraphs. If you are promoting your website, statistically, choosing Website conversions yields much better results than Website clicks.

Now that you have determined your Ad campaign type, you will be asked to select up to six different images. Be sure to at least include three different images to test different Ad variations, you should use A/B approach. Do not be afraid to test. Use big, eye catching images. Images are what increase your audience engagement the most.

You can choose three different methods to upload an image: you can upload an image from your PC, re-use a previously used Image, or browse images in Shutterstock (This is great if you want to keep things on the cheap side and find a high-quality picture, though if you want your Ad to be unique I would get my own pictures.)

Once you set up your image, you will be asked to set up the Ad's copy. This is probably the trickiest part of setting up your Ad.

Choosing the right words can bare a HUGE increase in engagement. Choose them wrong and your Ad will fail. Be sure to include the benefits of your product or service. Make people know how your product will help them. Provide value. You need to write copy for the title (25 characters long), description (90 characters) and news feed URL description (90 characters). As with the image, having different copy variations is really good. Test out! If you can offer a discount or something of the sort it is great to increase the amount of clicks you will get.

Ok, you now have your copy and image set up. You only need to determine the best placement for your Ad. You can choose between Mobile, right column, or news feed. Statistically, news feed Ads perform the best. However, as right column Ads are much cheaper, you can test out how well they perform.

Another thing to have in mind when choosing Mobile is to be careful to not lead the people clicking your Ad to a non-Mobile website. Otherwise you will have thrown your money down the toilet.

Determining Your Target Audience

This might be the most crucial step of creating your Ads. If you target your Ads wrongly you will get the wrong likes, "Cheap Likes", even if you get thousands of likes. You will not sell the same amount than if you target the correct audience. Also, the engagement rate will be much slower.

Demographic Ad Targeting

This way of targeting your Ads is the simplest out there. It is a pretty straight forward process. You will be able to choose between:

- **Location:** From country to zip codes. Be careful what you choose here. Depending what your product or service is and how much you want to spend you can choose the whole world or a "near you" ten-mile radius. Be wary that if you choose a large area you will get a lot of likes but it will be much more expensive. If you are promoting a coffee shop, you should target to a small radius near you. If you are offering a product that can be delivered anywhere in the US, choosing the whole US is a good idea as long as you can handle the costs.

- **Age:** Depending what your product or service is, you should choose between teenagers, young adults, people with families or retired people.
- **Gender:** When choosing gender, target specific genders. Nowadays, Facebook offers a huge selection of different genders. Up to fifty different ones! You can target different audiences depending what your product is. Be sure to change the copy and images for different genders. Males, for example, should be approached different than women.

Recently, Facebook added the option to pick your target audience even more specifically. You can set to target with people with certain political views, job titles, ethnicity, etc. When choosing your target be wary that some people might not have filled this type of information in your profile. You might end up narrowing your audience too much.

Interest Ad Targeting

This type of Ad targeting is the best one to use. It allows you to target people who are interested in your product or service particularly. For example, you can target people who are interested in your competitor's product or your market.

You will be able to choose between:

- **Precise Interests:** This type of targeting lets you target people based off their profile information. This targeting keeps targets people who have liked something related to your industry. Facebook will let you type different industries. Once you select the most appropriate one, Facebook will show you a list of other related industries you can add. Add more than one interest so that you don't narrow your audience too much.
- **Behavior targeting:** Facebook analyzes each profile actions using cookies. If someone is looking for protein powders and

then uses Facebook, he will probably get protein powders Ads. It does not always work great, but if it does it's the best. You are sure that people who see your Ad are actively interested in something similar to your product or service.

Connection Ad Targeting

This type of Ad targeting looks for people who already like your Page, who are friends with people who have liked your Page or people who have not liked your Facebook Page.

You can use this type of targeting, for example, if you have a Page with millions of likes and want to engage people who have not liked your page yet, Connection Ad Targeting is awesome.

You can also increase the engagement of your Page posts by targeting people who are friends with your "likers".

Custom Audience Ad Targeting

This may be the most powerful Ad targeting if you have a list of emails, phone numbers or profile IDs. This way you can now that the Ads will show to people who you know that have given you their information because they are interested. By using this way of targeting you can up sell new products, make newsletter subscribers clients, etc.

If used correctly, this targeting method will yield the highest conversion rate. For example, if you are focusing on lead generation or people subscribing to your newsletter, you can exclude people who you already have their email.

Analyzing How Successful your Ad Campaign Is

Once your Ad is already out there, you can check out how it is performing using Facebook Ad Manager. Here, you will be shown statistics of people who have clicked your Ad, how much each click costs, the whole campaign reach, the amount of money spent today, total amount of money spent so far, start and end date.

As you can see these statistics are pretty specific. You can analyze lots of things from these campaign stats. If you want to understand how your campaign is performing today, be sure to select stats from the last seven days! Otherwise, your metric and recent results will be harder to measure and understand.

Analyzing each campaign is easy: you just need to click on the list shown in Facebook Ad Manager. Here you can disable the campaign for a while, view click frequency and view the clicks over time your Ads received in a graph. The FREQUENCY of your campaign is really important to pay attention to. It tells you how many times a unique user has seen your Advertisement. It is important to analyze because the higher the number, the less eye catching your ad is. The user saw your Ad, let's say, fifteen times until he clicked on it. Ultimately, your costs will go up and the results will go down!

Chapter 5 Key Points

- Make your Ads pop with nice looking, eye-catching images.
- Craft your Ads copy attentively.
- Don't be afraid to test different Ad variations.
- Before creating any type of Ad you need to be sure about its purpose it will have so you can determine the Ad type you will use and the way to target it.
- Analyze your campaign statistics, change the Ad accordingly. Pay attention to the **Frequency** stat.

Chapter 6 How to Direct Facebook Traffic to a Website

In the last chapter we have seen how to drive traffic to your website using Ads. But, also, there are other ways to achieve an increase in your website's traffic. In this chapter you will learn different techniques to achieve higher website traffic through Facebook. Are you ready?

<u>Make Sure Your Website is Updated Regularly with New Content</u>

Imagine that someone enters a website you have linked through Facebook and all they can find is a bad looking landing page, that doesn't show the website's purpose, while showing posts from two years ago. People will just leave the page without even reading anything. And sure that they won't share the page with their friends, or comment on your posts about it. Be sure to post something useful at least once a week. Some ideas that might help you with coming up with new content are:

1. Post a tip about your niche weekly. It doesn't have to be too long. Just a couple of paragraphs and a nice looking image. Try to answer some questions that your customers might have about your service or product.
2. Post an article of top 10 articles about something related to your business. You can find them all around the web. You can even add a short paragraph describing what you liked about each article.
3. Post an interview with someone related to your niche. The interview can just be 5-10 questions you have sent the interviewee through your email account.

Not only this will benefit in driving more traffic from Google keyword (search engine indexing), but it will encourage people to subscribe to your newsletter and be more excited about your Facebook Page posts.

<u>Make it Easy to Share Your Website's Content to Facebook</u>

People reading your content might want to share your articles to Facebook. This will increase traffic as, basically, you are getting free advertisement. Their friends will see the content they have shared and probably will surf your website.

To do this you need to add Facebook share button to your website. Be sure to include it in a place where it is viewable and in every single article you publish. Make it simple.

Another way for making your website readers share your content to their Facebook is just reminding them at the end of your articles! For example, "Did you like this article? Feel free to share it to Facebook by just clicking the button below!"

Optimizing Your Facebook Profile

Make sure you include your website's link in other places of your Page. For example, in the About Us page of your Facebook Page, include different links to different sections of your website. You might describe what your product or service is about including your website's link where they can read further. "Our product offers porcelain tableware at the best market prices. Find out more at www.yourwebsite.com/moreinfo

Chapter 6 Key Points

- Don't be afraid to think out of the box, post your website's URL everywhere you can. Ads are not the only way to drive more traffic.
- Keep your website updated and include a share to Facebook button.

Conclusion

Congratulations! You now have the knowledge to start building and increasing your business' clients. Eventually, the use of Facebook will increase your sales exponentially. Remember to not be afraid to test different variations in everything: your Page, your Ad campaigns and your Group. Although my recommendations of what works better statistically varies, different businesses might get more benefits using other type of Ads.

Make your content interesting, don't act like a robot. Your clients are people with feelings. Remember this and put it into action. Think what you would like to see if you where on your customers' feed. What value does your product or service provide? What is in it for them? List your product or service benefits and be sure to let your customers know what they are.

As a network marketer, remember what your new salespeople or new clients want. If you were someone who wants to start selling for a network marketing business, what would you want to know? Probably you would be seeking for a company you can trust, a person you can look up to, testimonials, and make money. Think of these things and include them in your Ads, Page, Groups and Website. If you were a client, you would be seeking what most people look for: how valuable is the product or service? People are willing to take out their VISA if they see that your product or service can solve something for them, make them look prettier, etc.

I want you to pay attention to this psychological study which found out how human beings are programmed, in terms of what they desire. Called Life Force Eight, the desires are the following:

1. Survival, enjoyment of life, life extension.
2. Enjoyment of food and beverages.
3. Freedom from fear, pain, and danger.
4. Sexual companionship.
5. Comfortable living conditions.

6. To be superior, winning, keeping up with the Joneses.

7. Care and protection of loved ones.

8. Social approval.

Make sure everything you create appeals to this desires.

Take Action, Provide Value, And Earn Money!

www.ingramcontent.com/pod-product-compliance
Lightning Source LLC
Chambersburg PA
CBHW061230180526
45170CB00003B/1230